A PLACE FOR WINTER

Paul Tiulana's Story

A PLACE FOR WINTER
Paul Tiulana's Story

by VIVIAN SENUNGETUK

and PAUL TIULANA

THE CIRI FOUNDATION   Anchorage, Alaska

Publication of *A Place for Winter, Paul Tiulana's Story* is funded by
a grant from the Alaska Humanities Forum and The CIRI Foundation
on a matching basis with Alascom, Inc.

Photographs are by Father Bernard R. Hubbard, S.J., from the Hubbard
Photograph Collection, Santa Clara University Archives,
Santa Clara, California.

Map and back jacket photographs by Kathy Kiefer.

Designed and printed in the United States of America
by Meriden-Stinehour Press, Lunenburg, Vermont.

ISBN 0–938227–02–5

First printing 1987

Address inquiries to: The CIRI Foundation,
P.O. Box 93330, Anchorage, Alaska 99509-3330.

Contents

7 Introduction

SECTION ONE 9 They Called Me "Dad"

SECTION TWO 10 October Is Icy Month

SECTION THREE 15 The Ice Never Sleeps

SECTION FOUR 18 It Was Not Hard Work At All

SECTION FIVE 21 There Was Always Something Happening

SECTION SIX 23 "Take Your Seal To That Older Person"

SECTION SEVEN 24 The Medicine Man Was A Protector

SECTION EIGHT 29 Relationships

SECTION NINE 32 During The Second World War

SECTION TEN 34 I Proved Myself

38 Epilogue

42 Note

124 Bernard R. Hubbard, S.J.

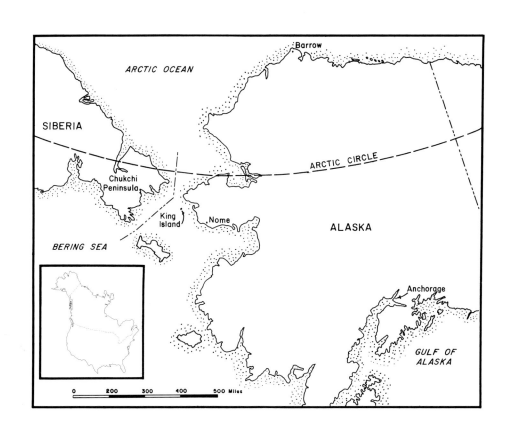

Introduction

I met Paul Tiulana in 1975 when he was invited to speak and dance at a Native arts conference in Sitka, Alaska. At that time I was working in Sitka as an education specialist for the Alaska Native Brotherhood, a fraternal Indian organization. The conference was an attempt at intercultural communication through the arts, and Paul contributed to its success. He was then and is now the recognized leader of the King Island Eskimo people who have relocated from the ancient village near Nome to the city of Anchorage. At the conference Paul proved to be an excellent, thoughtful speaker and a talented traditional Eskimo dancer.

From 1977 to 1980, Paul and I worked for the same human services organization in Anchorage, the Cook Inlet Native Association. He was employed as a cultural coordinator and I as a planner and fund-raiser. We sought each other's advice on numerous occasions.

Paul Tiulana is one of the great chiefs of traditional Eskimo people in Alaska today. He is a man who looks at the big picture and asks questions about what is happening around him. Remembering the past, he compares it with the present, analyzes changes and works for a better future. He is proud, sometimes to a fault. He takes care of his people in Anchorage and in Nome, advising them, securing work for them and protecting their interests in the white man's world as best he can. He looks for solutions to the problems of loss of identity and cultural conflict which affect his small group of first Americans and the larger population of Alaska Native people.

Paul has little academic education but he is a natural story-teller with a wide English vocabulary. One day I suggested to him that we put his story in print. He liked the idea. So in 1978 and 1979 we sat down together whenever we had a few minutes to spare. He remembered parts of his childhood and youth and we tape recorded everything. I asked a few questions but not a great many. During the summer of 1979 I had the time to transcribe the tapes and organize the resulting script in chronological order. The narrative that follows is Paul's own story of his people, edited only slightly for grammar and style.

Recently Paul and I became aware of the collection of photographs taken by Father Bernard R. Hubbard, a Jesuit explorer who lived on King Island in 1938 and 1939. Paul had mentioned Father Hubbard in his narrative. The collection is housed in the Archives of Santa Clara University. We were assisted in our contacts with the Archives by Father Louis Renner, a Jesuit scholar in Fairbanks. Paul sorted through hundreds of pictures taken by this extraordinary photographer, identifying almost every face, even the faces of babies. We chose forty pictures to illustrate Paul's autobiography.

There were less than 200 people on King Island when Father Hubbard visited. He took hundreds of pictures. He must have taken many pictures of every individual there. Still, it seems fortuitous that the collection contains the lovely pictures of Paul, his mother, his sister, his uncles and cousins, and his young wife that illustrate this story. Paul and I think that the book was meant to be.

Anchorage, 1987   VIVIAN SENUNGETUK

They Called Me "Dad"

My name is Paul Tiulana. I am from King Island. King Island is in the Bering Sea, northwest of Nome, Alaska. We Eskimos have lived there as long as anybody can remember. Our Eskimo name for King Island is Ooq-vok which means "place for winter." It is a rocky place and steep. We built our houses on stilts because there was no flat place on the sides of the island.

I was born sixty-five years ago, before any white man had lived on King Island. They named me Tiulana, after my grandfather. That is my Eskimo name. I did not get the name Paul until I was baptized. The priest gave me the name Paul. That is my Christian name and everybody calls me Paul now.

I can remember back to when I was seven or eight years old, what the older folks said to me. In living I was taught to be respectful to others. I was taught to follow all the rules about living in the village, so that I would be a respected person in the future. You see, if I did not help the older folks, they would be inclined not to help me, because I did not obey the rules. The more I obeyed their counseling, the more they gave me their ideas as I grew up. Every day counseling came from my uncles and aunts and my grandfathers. Also my cousins had to counsel me.

If we obeyed the older persons, they made us toys for being obedient. They gave us anything that we wanted when they saw that we were going to be really obedient persons, even if it was hard to make. My father made a bow and arrow for me. In the springtime, about April, when the snowbirds came to King Island, we used to hunt them with bows and arrows. And every time we killed a little bird, we put a little notch in the bow, so we could tell how many birds we killed year to year. Mom cooked the birds for us. I had to be obedient for the older persons and they made me the really good arrows that I wanted.

I lost my father when I was nine. He went out hunting on the ice and never came back. From then on my Uncle Olanna, my dad's brother, called me "Dad." Everybody called me "Dad" even though I was a little boy.

I had quite a few relatives who counseled me when they visited my mother, so that everything would be good for me in the future. Uncle Panatok, one of the respected persons to me, was second cousin to my father. He would come to our house and ask me, "Did your mother spank you this morning, or say some hard words to you?"

Even if my mother had not spanked me, I would say that she had. Then my uncle would go to my mother and say, "Do not scold your son!" You see, on the family tree, the way they were related, my uncle and my mother were supposed to tease each other. They were what we called cross-cousins. That made my uncle my right-hand man. He told my mother not to scold me. "When you hurt Dad's feelings, you hurt *my* feelings," he would say to her. So even when my mother had not spanked me, my uncle's teasing of her would give me a little comfort.

SECTION TWO 🐋 *October Is Icy Month*

At King Island we lived by the weather. We had certain activities every month and we named the months according to the activities and the weather.

I will start with October. The name for October in the King Island dialect of the Eskimo language is "icy month." We call it "icy month" because ice starts to form below the village among the rocks at this time. Ice starts to form from the bottom of the Bering Sea.

We call November "going up to the back of the island and hunt there." There is a long Eskimo word that means that. November is the month when the wind starts blowing really hard from the north, blowing ice into the island on the north side and out from the island on the south side. The ice is not anchored down around the south side of the island and it is not safe enough to try to walk there. The ones who have walked there have drifted out on the young ice and have never come back. They drowned out in the water when the wind started blowing hard from the north and waves crushed the ice in the Bering Sea.

We did not walk too far away from the island in any direction, unless we carried kayaks with us in the fall of the year. November was "going up to the back of the island and hunt there" because it was safer to hunt on the back, or north, side of King Island then. We mostly worked on our furs then, so that we could have new mukluks, or boots, new seal pants, new parkas, or coats. We renewed some of the hunting equipment that had to be used in the winter time.

December we call "dancing month." We started to dance in December because everything on King Island was ready for winter. Our houses were ready. We had put away our skin boats up in racks. We had stored our things for the winter so that we did not have to worry about them anymore. We danced in the month of December and through the winter, some old songs and some new ones. We prepared new songs for the show we put on for other Eskimo people on the mainland in the summer.

January we call "reverse dance month." The people on King Island say that long ago they tapped the drums with the opposite hand in January. I do not know why they did it. I have never seen it but I have been told that it was done that way.

The older men were hunting mostly seal and polar bear in January. When a hunter got a polar bear, an old person told a story while the women cleaned the skin. We ate the meat and saved the skin. We made a hole down in the ice and put the skin down in it. The little shrimps in the water ate the blood and excess fat from the skin. We let the skin stay down there maybe a couple of days. Then we kids pulled it out, cleaned it off with snow and squeezed the salt water from the hair. And after we did this, we used to take it up on the hill and slide down on the skin. There were about a dozen children riding on that bear skin; we slid down over and over until just before sundown. Then the hunter who got the polar bear skin came and rolled up the skin and put it underneath his skin boat until March.

The older persons also hunted seals in January. When they got a one year old seal, they tried to use the skin to make sealskin pants, because the fur is a bit longer on a young seal and the pants would last longer. They used the skin of a female seal to make mukluks (boots) and mittens. The skin of a female seal is lighter. When they killed an older male seal, they worked to bleach the skin. The bleached sealskin was used to make parkas, or coats. They put the skin in the water for about three days, then pulled it out after rinsing off the excess fat. Then they put the skin outside on a rack in front of the house and let it freeze during the night. Bleached skins were left outside in the winter to cure and dry.

The month of February is "the month of the prematurely born seal." Sometimes the seal miscarries in the month of February. In February the older men were mostly out hunting. The sealskin is prime during the months of January and February.

The month of March we call "fixing our kayaks for springtime." In the month of March we repaired everything on our kayaks. We renewed our harpoons, renewed our harpoon lines. If we did not want to change the skin on our kayaks, we applied blubber over the skins. It had to be done only a couple of times because the third time we could burn the skin. If we put too much oil on the skin, it started to get soft and easy to tear. In March we tried to get everything ready for the spring hunt.

April is the "month for going out hunting with our kayaks." That is what the King Island Eskimo word for that time of year means. As soon as the seals are born the first part of April, the ice stops forming around the island. It does not freeze anymore. When that happened we went out with our kayaks, mostly for oogruks, or big bearded seals.

Towards the end of April we started to see some walrus on top of the ice, coming from the south. It was an exciting time. The men hardly slept. Maybe they slept about two or three hours at night and woke up to go hunting. The days started to get longer in April as the sun rose earlier in the morning and set later at night.

Even in the month of April we still danced once in a while. Whenever the weather was bad, sometimes we danced for the weather to calm down, because we did not have much to do. We tried to do something by dancing, to kill time. Sometimes when we danced to make the weather good, we timed it right and the weather *was* good the next day. It is true that even outdoors we danced for the weather to be good. It happened even in my days.

One time we had weather from the north blowing for a couple of weeks. The men were kind of curious, kind of disappointed. One night they said they were going to dance for the weather. They danced all night and in about three days the weather was good — maybe something like praying.

The month of May we call "the ice starts to melt from the island." The first part of May we were still trying to hunt for oogruks, or big bearded seals, with our kayaks, because we did not have to walk. It is easier to get the big bearded seals with kayaks, not walking. We brought in more meat in May, put the seals in our kayaks, and when we reached land, dragged them with our sleds.

Towards the end of May we started going out for walruses. Also we rebuilt our skin boats. We made new frames and covered the skin boats with new skins. We had two kinds of boats at King Island — kayaks and skin boats. The kayaks were one-man canoes, lightweight. Skin boats were large, maybe thirty feet long and six feet wide, and heavy, made with driftwood frames covered by split walrus hides. After the ice began to scatter, we started to use the skin boats because they were safer than kayaks in open water, out hunting. Maybe a sudden storm came up and we had a long way to paddle. It could be done but we preferred to hunt with the skin boat when the ice was scattering. We could bring more meat with the skin boat. At this time we hardly slept.

A long time ago, when they were working on the meat that the hunters brought in, the ladies slept on the rocks because they did not have time to walk back and forth to the houses. They would have wasted time going back and forth. They cut the meat on the rocks and slept there, too. The older girls took care of the young children in the houses. Only after they finished their cutting did the ladies go back to their homes.

We call the month of June "unnoticed moon." In June everything was so busy that we did not have time to think what day it was. We worked on preparing our walrus meat — putting it in the caves for preservation — so that we would have more meat for next year. We worked so hard that we did not notice the month. We hardly thought about anything but working on the walrus meat and skins.

July is the month of "going over to the mainland." We went over to the mainland in our skin boats, to see our friends there, to trade with them and to dance. We practiced new dances in the winter to show them in the summer. It was a sort of contest to see who could make up the best dance.

Before we left the island in the month of July we were picking some greens that had to be preserved during the summer for their winter uses. There were four plants that we put in seal oil; they were preserved in that oil and they did not spoil at all. We made Eskimo ice cream with one plant. It was done like this: A container was made out of walrus hide and the plant was pounded with a walrus tusk while the plant was still frozen. It was then mixed with reindeer fat and seal oil. We used it when we were eating seal or oogruk. Delicious!

We do not have a name for the month of August. We were still on the mainland then. We were picking berries — blackberries, blueberries, salmon-berries. I would call August "berry-picking month."

September we call "ready to go back to the island." We were thinking of going back to the island while the weather was good because in the fall of the year, in the month of October, the Bering Sea gets really rough. We tried to go back to the island in the month of September so that we would have time to winterize our houses.

SECTION THREE *The Ice Never Sleeps*

When I was about ten years old, my uncles and my older brother taught me how to survive out on the ice when I was out hunting. They taught me what I had to do with my clothes, what I had to do when I went out hunting by myself, and what the weather would do to me if I drifted out from King Island on the ice. You see, the ice forms on the Bering Sea all around the island, but the ocean underneath is always moving. They taught me all the survival techniques that I would have to utilize when I drifted out on the moving ice. They said, "The ice never sleeps; the current never sleeps."

Sometimes my uncle trained me, just constantly walking all day long without stopping at all. He wanted to build my body to run long distances without stopping. I even had to hold my breath for long distance walking.

That is one of the survival techniques we worked on. We were not supposed to smoke when we were young because smoking is bad for your breath. You get exhausted maybe in fifteen minutes if you smoke early. Walking while holding your breath builds your lungs for long distance running.

If we were hunting south of the island and the north wind started to blow, we had to start running. The wind from the north pushes the ice away from the south of the island and the sea opens up. If we lost our breath and stopped in five minutes, there would be an open lead, open water, between us and the island. We would not be able to cross it. We had to run constantly, maybe five miles, maybe ten miles, until we reached a safe point, without stopping at all and carrying our hunting bags. Everything about us had to be prepared for our survival.

I was taught by my Uncle Olanna. He took me out when I was eleven years old and taught me how the currents moved around the island. He taught me the direction of the wind to the island. Right in front of King Island there is shore ice and there are some rocks and big boulders sticking out from the shore ice. He told me to mark the rocks, to line up objects with my eyes. Then if we drifted too far, we could look for the markers on the rocks and we would know which way to walk to be in a safe place.

One day my Uncle Olanna took me out on the ice for two or three hours to hunt seals. I was a really bad shot: I missed every time when a seal came up. He got frustrated with me and took me back to the village. Then he went out again to get some seals himself. That is the way I was taught when I was young.

Even the ladies had to teach me some hunting techniques, things that had been said to them by their fathers when they were small. They tried to explain to me what their fathers had told them about hunting survival. I never read those things; they were not written down. I had to memorize them by heart.

I was taught another thing by my mother. She said, "Son, there are two barrels out in the shed that used to be filled by your father, filled just full of blubber." She encouraged me to be like my father. My father was one of the great hunters at King Island and I wanted to be like him. I tried every way to be like my father. Even though I got really tired with tears in my eyes, I tried to keep up with the others out hunting.

I was taught not to take a nap during the day because in the future, when I grew up, I would be infected with sleepiness during the day. If I went out hunting and stayed out a couple of days, then rode in my kayak, I could get sleepy and tip over. So whenever I lay down, my Uncle Akilena called me and said, "Dad, get up! You'd better not take a nap. It is not good for you." And even though I was really sleepy, I would try to get up and do something.

The next step, when I was about sixteen, was to learn how to ride on a kayak, a one-man canoe. My uncle taught me. We practiced how to ride it in the spring time when the ice was all gone from the island and the weather was good, calm. Sometimes I asked my uncle if I could ride a kayak. He said, "Go ahead, as long as somebody goes with you. If you tip over and there is nobody around, you will drown."

Going out hunting in a kayak is something else. In the spring, when the people of the village spotted walrus, the men started out fast. The walrus are very heavy to pull behind the kayaks, so the hunters tried to reach them as close to the island as possible, right in sight of the island. In the spring when they started to go out hunting for walrus, the older hunters never stopped. They constantly paddled hard for the herd of walrus. If they drifted out too far from the island, it would take more hours to get back, but if they reached the herd close in, the current would push them back to the island. They would have less distance to go over the shore ice.

One time they started to go out at two o'clock in the morning. This was in May when the sun never sets. I had had only one or two hours of sleep.

This was my first experience walrus hunting with the older persons and it was a good thing that I had a thermos bottle of coffee with me. The older men constantly paddled hard and I tried to follow them. My uncle had taught me to paddle with my kayak but I was getting very tired. Finally, during the riding, they stopped and climbed up on a pressure ridge of ice to look around for about ten minutes. I reached for my coffee and got a little zip to moisten my mouth. It kept me going. They went on in their kayaks and somehow I kept up with them, about fifteen older men.

We got about ten walrus that day. When I got home my mother was really glad because I could follow the older hunters. She said I was ready for anything.

SECTION FOUR 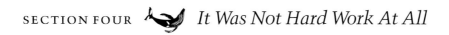 *It Was Not Hard Work At All*

When I was growing up at King Island, it was not hard work at all. I just enjoyed life because that is the way that I was brought up. It was really hard work but magically I did not feel it. I went out hunting all day long, and I got really tired when I came in. When I slept I got all rested up. I did not have feelings of tiredness. When I woke up I was ready to go out again whenever the weather was good.

I had to learn to make many things, to hunt and to survive out in the ice. Out on King Island we did not know what was going to happen in another three hours if we were walking out in the ice. If we did not have the right equipment, we would be lost. We would be dead.

Most of our equipment we carried in a hunting bag. The hunting bag was made from an old sealskin that had been used as a float for a couple of years. A new sealskin could be sewn up and filled with air and used to help float dead oogruks and walruses along to the island. After a couple of years the skin was not good enough to float anymore because the pores had been opened on it, but it was weatherized. Then it was good for a hunting bag. We had to have a weatherized hunting bag when the weather was bad, rain and snow mixed. If it were not weatherized, it would get wet and be much heavier.

The hunting bag was about three feet long and about two feet wide. We carried the hunting bag on the back with a strap over the chest. If we fell in the water we could take it off fast. We did not have any buckles at all. Also the same with the rifle case. It just had one strap with no buckles. We put the gun in the case so that we just had to swing it around and pull the gun out. If we were walking along the open water and all of a sudden a seal came up—maybe this is the last seal we would see in a day—we had to get the gun in a real hurry.

On the back of the hunting bag we had two straps so that we could tie snowshoes on the bag. If we sat down on the ice by the open water, we used the hunting bag as a cushion. We used snowshoes as a protection under the hunting bag so that it did not get wet.

To make the snowshoes we had to find a four inch by four inch willow tree growing out in the tundra or on a hillside. We cut one piece about two lengths of our arms and that would be about the right length for the frame of the snowshoes. We used hand measurements for making holes on the sides of the frame. Hand measurements are exact measurements. Our snowshoes were very small because the snow at King Island is more compact than the snow out on the mainland. If you are walking out by the trees on the mainland, the snow is soft. On the mainland they have to use bigger snowshoes. At King Island our snowshoes were mostly for walking on slush ice.

For the rawhide bindings on the snowshoes, we had to use spotted seal because it is much stronger than the regular common sealskin. On the top part of the snowshoes we had to use the common sealskin because it is much thinner.

Inside the hunting bag we carried a long piece of oogruk hide about two inches wide and another line a half inch wide. These we could attach to a seal and drag it. We also had another rope in case it was required for emergency uses. If we killed a seal or a polar bear, we had to bind it with lines, so we kept a good mixture of lines in our hunting bags. So that we did not have to carry extra weight in our hunting bags, we measured the lines with our arms.

We also had a raincoat in the hunting bag at all times. It was a main item of our survival gear. If I fell in the water and stayed for five minutes, my parka would get wet. As soon as it got frozen it would stand away from my body and not maintain body heat. If this happened I had to put the raincoat on under the parka and tie the string around my waist. By the heat of my body the parka would be dried slowly. The raincoat was made of either big bearded seal intestine or walrus intestine.

Also in the hunting bag we carried an extra bundle of hay, to use as extra insoles for our mukluks. If we fell in the water and the water got inside our mukluks, we had to change the insoles. We always used hay. We did not use felt insoles when we went out hunting because the hay was lighter.

We always carried a piece of walrus intestine about one foot long. Whenever we got really thirsty we put snow inside of the intestine and put it under our parka; the heat of our body melted the snow. Then we had water to drink. We did not just eat snow. If you swallow snow you will get gas. If you do not have water, slush is good. You can let the slush melt inside your mouth and drink from it a little bit. The rest is thrown out because the gas develops inside you stomach and it is not good.

I have been taught how to obtain water. If I were to be away from the island and I were walking on thin ice — there is no snow on the new ice — I could make a little hole in the ice. The first water that came up I could drink because it is not too salty. Underneath the thin ice there is a little bit of fresh water between the ice and the salt water. Not more than one mouthful.

We only wore one t-shirt and the parka when we went out hunting. If we wore too many clothes when we dragged the seal, we got exhausted quickly. A fur parka was all we needed. Our body heat had to escape from the body. We carried an extra shirt in our hunting bag for sleeping on the ice.

SECTION FIVE *There Was Always Something Happening*

I had to learn hunting procedures from my uncles and my older brother. I had to do things in a certain way to learn from the older people. I learned about each animal, the way it could be approached and killed, and how it should be handled for use later. There was always something happening.

Probably we Eskimos know more about the animals around King Island than the modern society knows. We know the sound the oogruk, or big bearded seal makes when it goes down into the water in the spring time, in the month of March. It makes about four notes and sounds like a musical instrument far down in the ocean. They say the sounds are either for eating or mating. We could hear the sounds about a mile away when we were out hunting in our kayaks. We used our paddles — put them in the water and listened to them — to try to pinpoint where the sounds came from. Then we timed our paddling to the sounds. As the big bearded seal made the sounds, we stroked quickly, twice on one side, twice on the other side. When the seal makes the sounds, he cannot hear at all. If we used our paddles after the seal made the sounds, he would be disturbed very easily.

There would be bubbles coming up from the water and the big bearded seal would always come up near the bubbles. If we disturbed the animal, that would be the last time we saw him. We had to approach the seal very quietly.

When the seal came up, we had to sit still. When we were near enough, we used a harpoon.

We did not always hunt the oogruk with our kayaks. Sometimes we went out on foot, in the winter time. Each hunter would cover a different area. If a hunter found a breathing hole, he would signal the other people in the area by making a big circle with one arm. If he shouted the seal would hear him. If it were a common seal hole, the hunter would pat his leg. If it were a big bearded seal hole, an oogruk hole, he would pat his head. We had to know those two signals.

Whenever somebody killed a big bearded seal on the ice, he would make a loud sound. There would be other alert hunters around the area. When the other hunters heard the signal, they would know an oogruk had been killed. All the hunters in the area would run toward the hunter who had killed the big bearded seal. The seal was divided among all the hunters who ran in to help. The first person who got in to the hunter got the breast meat; the second and third got the hindquarters; the fourth and fifth got the frontquarters; the sixth got the spinal bones; the seventh got neck bones; and the eighth got the skull. The hunter got the ribs and lower part of the vertebrae.

The big bearded seal weighs about seven hundred pounds and about five men would be needed to pull one in. The meat was divided out on the ice. We carried in our hunting bags a small part of the walrus stomach to use as a container for meat. That way we did not get our hunting bags messed up. There is always some blood that drains out of the animal. The blood could be scraped up from the snow and put into the walrus stomach. When we got home we would boil the snow and make it into soup.

"Take Your Seal To That Older Person"

If we killed any kind of animal for the first time, we had to give it away to an older person. This was the Eskimo way. There was a story about a hunter a long time ago who got a seal. He did not want anybody to touch it. It was the only seal he killed in his lifetime. From this story we learned that we had to give our first animal away, no matter how valuable it was. My first walrus, my first common seal, my first big bearded seal, my first polar bear—I had to give them away. The common seal and birds we gave to one person. Same with the big bearded seal. The walrus we shared.

My uncle picked who I would give an animal to. If there were an older person hunting nearby, I had to take the animal to that person. When I got my first seal we noticed this older person nearby and my uncle told me, "Take your seal to that older person." If there were nobody around, we had to take the animal to the village and my uncle named the older person that I would give the skin and the meat to. We considered a person older when he did not go out hunting much anymore.

About one week after the hunt our relatives had to give a dance for that animal that we killed. They said, "That animal you killed is going to vomit more birds and animals for you in later years." That is what the dancing was for, to make a young man a successful hunter.

We also had to learn the cloud formations. My uncle taught me. In winter time there are snow crystals when it starts to get cold. When we saw snow crystals coming down from the clouds, that meant it was going to be windy later on. Also we could tell where there was open water when the weather was cloudy. Above the open water we could see a dark, sort of black, cloud.

When I was hunting one spring with my uncle, I made a big mistake. There is a way to set a harpoon and harpoon line on top of a kayak. There are two bindings right on top of the kayak. There is a seal poke that floats and a line is attached. That line is supposed to be put underneath the two bindings. Whenever the hunter spears a seal, all he has to do is just pull the animal in and throw the seal poke. What I did was put the line underneath the bindings so that I could not pull it out. I speared the seal and tried to pull it in. Instead it pulled me. I knew that I had done something wrong. The seal pulled on the line and broke it; I lost the seal and I lost my harpoon.

When we got to the shore ice, I told my uncle about it. That was the day. He really gave me some hard words. I could have been pulled over in my kayak and drowned. My uncle did not want to see me just like my father. He did not want me to drown out there. He taught me everything I needed to know to survive because my dad never came back from hunting. He gave me some hard words for my survival. He did not say anything bad. He said, "You *have* to do it the right way." After that I looked twice before I attached my harpoon line to the seal poke.

SECTION SEVEN *The Medicine Man Was A Protector*

In the way of religion I would compare King Island beliefs with the religion of the Old Testament. We sacrificed some game in order to have more game in the future. If I killed a little bird for the first time, my relatives skinned it, saved the skin and hung it up. Then they had some kind of a dance to honor the bird. This was to encourage me to be a successful hunter, saying that the little bird would vomit more game for me in the future.

When we killed any kind of animal, we honored it. Like the polar bear; the hunter put a little bit of water inside its mouth so it could drink, so another bear could come back the next year. There was no big sermon to honor the bear, just a little ceremony in order to get more animals in the future for the village.

We had medicine men and women to cure the sick, to find some lost articles, and to protect the village from unknown, powerful demons that would be coming in during the dances at night. The medicine man was a protector. He could see a demon right away and make it go away. Otherwise the demon would destroy some of the villagers.

When a demon appeared at the clubhouse in our village at night, where we were dancing, the medicine man automatically had the power. He would go into a trance in the clubhouse. Then he would beat the Eskimo drum and scare the demon away.

They used to say that if any kind of a spirit wanted to come into a house, there would be a big bang on top of the house. Then when the spirit started to come in, a fog would come in first and the seal oil lamp would flicker. There is a story about two young children who stayed at their house during the dances one night. There was a big bang on top of their house and the children were really scared because they had been told about demons. They knew right away. A fog came in the entrance way of their house, then a spirit. It was their grandfather who was dead, coming in as a human. But he came in backwards, not showing his face. He said, "There is a big, scary demon waiting to come into your house, so I came to protect you."

The spirit in the form of their grandfather stayed all evening to protect the children. After the dances were over, the parents came home. They slipped on the stairs, maybe on the demon. The spirit flew up and away, right through the walls of the house. The children tried to follow the spirit of their grandfather but they hit against the wall instead of going through it and came back to their parents.

The medicine men did good things for the village. They cured the sick and found lost objects. Also they danced for good weather. Same thing with the women. They were comparable in their power with the men. The medicine men and women travelled up in space, their souls travelled, their spirits travelled. This power occurred in certain persons. They say that if a person liked to have that power, he or she could accept it. If a person did not want to use the power, he or she could reject it. A medicine man or woman had to perform to demonstrate the power. There were stories about medicine men and women from different villages competing with each other. They swallowed things, whatever was around, to demonstrate their powers. If a person were sick the medicine man or woman had to have a drum, an Eskimo drum, to perform. Or an intestine raincoat could do it also, so that the medicine person could be possessed by the spirit. All the villagers had to be in their houses because a medicine person could not get the power if anyone were stepping on the snow or the ground outside. The medicine men and women performed mostly at night when people were in their houses.

The medicine men knew when any hunter drifted away from the island. They knew because they heard a loud crack on the house of the hunter's relatives. If they heard a loud crack on the top of the relative's house, that meant the hunter was all right; everything was okay. But if the loud crack came underneath the house, that meant the hunter was dead.

In 1949, three men drifted out from King Island and only one came back. One of the men who was lost was my third cousin, Pahina. His grandparents noticed that there was a loud crack underneath their house and they knew right away that he was dead. Another of the men who was out on the ice was named Ayac. In his house his extra pair of dry boots, or mukluks, was hanging on a rafter up in the ceiling. His mother watched them during the night when everyone was sleeping. If the mukluks went back and forth just a little bit, that meant the hunter was still alive. Father Cunningham, our priest, even came to the house and blessed the mukluks, so that any demons would be chased away. And it happened that the mukluks were still moving. Ayac survived, after being lost for seventeen days in the Chukchi Sea. Seventeen days!

We had a Catholic church on King Island from the early 1920's. Father LaFortune came in the early 1920's and after people on King Island saw and heard him, they believed in the Catholic Church. In 1938 Father Hubbard came to visit King Island and to take pictures of us and the island. He put a "Christ the King" statue on top of the island and demons were never heard again.

The Northland, a United States Coast Guard ship, brought the "Christ the King" in the spring. It is a bronze statue about five feet tall, made on the East Coast. Of course it was heavy. All the men on King Island made a long line along a rope and they pulled it up. Every time the men on the side lifted the statue, the men above pulled it. It took almost a day to do it because it was so heavy and everybody got tired. The islanders were really pleased about having the "Christ the King" because maybe ten years prior an old person had dreamed about it. He said he dreamed that a really shiny thing had come down from the sky and landed where the "Christ the King" statue was to be placed.

Before the "Christ the King" statue was brought to the island, we had unusual activities, unexplained activities caused by a demon. Long ago, before I was born, maybe before Christianity existed, a woman fell down on the east side of the island and died. She became a demon, a really strong demon. And whenever she wanted to play with a person, a hunter, she caused the land and the sea to vibrate. Everything was vibrating when she hollered underneath the water. And the hunter could see all kinds of game — walrus, bears, seals, whales, all kinds of birds. And the mainland seemed to be only about a mile away when it was really thirty-five miles away. The demon would appear at the top of the island and glide down into the water. A second later she would appear again at the top. In the winter time she had a breathing hole in the ice and if a hunter saw one little hair of her head through the breathing hole, she started to holler and then attacked him. She killed three of her brothers long ago.

After a hunter had seen the demon, as he returned to the village, he forgot everything about what had happened, unless he started to bleed. Then a person could ask him, "What happened to you? You're bleeding." Then the hunter remembered everything that had happened. You see, the demon had caused him to bleed because she was so powerful. Also, maybe he was bleeding from exhaustion.

After the "Christ the King" was placed on top of the island, the demon's activities completely stopped. We were not afraid anymore. Christianity brought security to us. Before that the medicine men were security for the village.

Some of the other villages, on other islands and on the mainland, reported a glow over the island after the statue went up. People on Little Diomede Island and in Wales and Teller saw it sometimes in the 1940's. They thought the whole village might be burning. It still glows at night sometimes, even now when there is nobody out there. It is unexplainable, beyond my knowledge.

An older person on King Island once was telling me about a medicine man long before Christianity who said that this universe has a creator. He said that if you eat the flesh and drink the blood of this universe's creator, you will be safe. This was before anyone on King Island had heard anything about Christianity.

Relationships

When I was a child on King Island I was poor because my father had died. But as I got older I started to get some things. I learned to hunt, I had the best hunting equipment made for me by my uncles, I was physically fit. I started to feel that I could take anything. I could do anything. There was nothing in my field that I could not do, because I had been trained to take care of myself and I had a lot of exercise.

Then my mother remarried. I liked my step-father but he had a mother-in-law that I hated. You see, he lost his first wife but he still had his first wife's mother coming to visit him. She would come into our house, nagging at my mother, even though my mother did not do anything wrong. I had really bad feelings about this woman because she upset my mother. Sometimes my mother cried.

My step-father did not do anything because she was his in-law. We could not say anything to in-laws. It was not allowed in the Eskimo way. No matter what our in-laws did, we could not say anything. I felt that I wanted to do something physically to that woman, maybe knock her down.

Finally that woman died but I did not forget her. When I was about nineteen I said something about her in the clubhouse, in front of my uncle. My uncle was the brother-in-law of the woman who caused our family problems. I said, "I wish that woman were alive right now. When she came into the clubhouse, I would throw her out into the cold."

I looked at my uncle and he gave me a really bad eye. I forgot about it soon but he told my cousin to talk to me. My cousin told me (from my uncle really) that when a poor person starts to get something, he becomes hard to other people. My uncle saw right away that I was starting to do something bad, because I had been poor and I was beginning to have something. He told my cousin to tell me a story indirectly so that I would get the idea that I was starting to make problems within myself and for the village. I understood right away and I stopped.

Our behavior was controlled by relationships. When a person was bad, when a person started to make problems for another person, relationships came in. Maybe his cousin or his uncle would tell him not to do it, the first time. They gave him another chance.

Cross-cousins were very important in our culture. When a man and a wife had a son and daughter, the son's children were cross-cousins with the daughter's children. If the family had two boys and one girl, the two boys' children were partner's cousins. They were cross-cousins to the one girl's children. Same way if there were two daughters and one son. The two girls' children were partner's cousins and they were cross-cousins to the one boy's children.

It is very confusing. My mother and my aunt told me at a young age who were my partner's cousins and who were my cross-cousins. I do not really know the history of how the system came about but it really united our village government. That is how our village government controlled, with cross-cousins and partner's cousins. Cross-cousins were supposed to tease each other, to make fun of each other when somebody did something wrong. Partner's cousins were supposed to help each other throughout life.

Cross-cousins could make any kind of jokes, try to make each other feel bad. And if a person lost his temper because of something a cross-cousin said, he would be called a bad apple. Whenever someone misbehaved or did something foolish, someone would tell his cross-cousin about it and the cross-cousin would tease, make up jokes or songs to make the person feel funny. This went on throughout life.

Partner's cousins would stick together, talk to each other and work together. If a person got in trouble, a partner's cousin would feel badly about it. If one partner's cousin thought the other one were causing a problem for someone else, he would not say anything directly. He would not call a partner's cousin a problem to his face. He would tell a cross-cousin about it and the cross-cousin would do all he or she could to make the problem person feel funny.

People knew, they observed, whether a person were bad or not. A lot of times they gave a person a second chance, a third chance. They tried to make some kind of a relationship with a problem person. They could not just ignore the person because he or she would become more of a problem.

Sometimes things happened. A person had a big mouth and made things hard for another person, over and over. Finally the trouble-maker would be killed. Nobody would care. People would say, "He asked for it." When a murder happened, the uncle of the murdered person, or some other relative, could decide to take revenge, maybe kill the murderer. He could do this to satisfy himself, but this upset the village further. If the person who was killed was bad anyway, the people would say, "He asked for it." There would be no really hard feelings in the village.

Mostly we used our dancing to try to take out our frustrations that we had among ourselves. If we did not have anything to do, because the weather was bad, we got frustrated. Dancing, singing and laughing with each other cured the frustrations of our people. Take the person who lost his wife and was depressed and did not want to be helped. His cousin or his grandfather would tell him, "You should go over and join the dances. You are going, going down, trying to bring back the memory of your wife. You might as well go over and join the dances." So he did that and he forgot the bad things, and a couple of weeks later he was all right. His mind could think of something besides the loss.

During The Second World War

People on King Island did not know what was happening in the world. We did not have the political knowledge to try to understand other places.

We had radios at King Island and the teachers had a two-way radio. Whenever we wanted to report from King Island, we called Nome on the two-way radio; and when people in Nome had news, they called King Island. Sometimes we sent some telegrams to our relatives to ask them how they were and they answered back. That is how we got news from outside, by two-way radio. We had a schedule for calling in the morning and in the afternoon. If the reception was bad in the morning, we called in the afternoon.

During the Second World War there were two guys on King Island who understood a little bit about English. They wrote down what the news was and gave the information to our priest, Father LaFortune. He was a white priest, French Canadian, but he spoke English and he spoke Eskimo like us. He was with the King Island people for maybe fifteen years or more. He lived in a little house all by himself. He ate just like us. He spoke just like us. He gave half the sermon in Eskimo. He told us what was happening in the Second World War.

We did not understand what was wrong, why countries were fighting each other. What was the cause? What was the reason that they were fighting? We did not have the knowledge to try to understand these problems.

A lot of times people would say, "What the heck are they doing, fighting each other, killing people? They cannot eat human beings. They should come here to Alaska and hunt some animals for their food." That was the reaction that I used to hear from the older folks at King Island. "How come they kill each other? They cannot eat the bodies of the human beings they kill."

I was drafted into the army during the Second World War. I spoke a little bit of English. I was Class A when I went into the Army. Same way with some others; there were quite a few men from the village that passed the medical examination. The ones that really did not understand English were not drafted, and those who were too old or had medical problems were not drafted. I was sent to Nome for basic training. Some were sent out of Alaska, over towards Japan. Other than that most of us were stationed in Alaska. One of the King Island boys was stationed in Dutch Harbor in the Aleutian Islands when the Japanese bombed the town. He said he was really scared because he could hear the bombs whistling down.

One summer the people on King Island saw Japanese artillery in the area. There was one man walking on top of the island and he saw the boat coming in. He went to warn the villagers. They waited and waited and waited but nothing happened. It was a submarine that went down before getting to the village. They never saw it again.

It is very hard to land a boat at King Island. There is no sand bar to land on; there are only boulders. Even though we had been at King Island through-out our lifetimes, we had to look for the right place to land sometimes. We had to land in seconds, before the breakers came in. If we did not pull the boat out of the water right away, the waves would break the boat. Anyone who did not know how to land would lose his boat. So it was not likely that King Island could be attacked by sea.

Only one bush pilot ever landed a plane on the island. He landed on top of the island, going uphill. Taking off he just slid down the hill. This guy was a really good pilot I would say. He said that it was no problem landing on King Island. The only way for a plane to land most of the time was on the shore ice. Sometimes we made a temporary landing strip down on the shore ice. We moved rocks and snow to make a flat runway. There were a few bush pilots who knew how to land on the shore ice.

We were ready for any kind of action at King Island. We had our army rifles, we were trained. Everyone knew how to shoot at King Island anyway. We did not have to train, except maybe for a surprise attack. We knew the island just like the palms of our hands. If the Japanese had ever tried to get into King Island we knew what to do , where to hide, how to sleep on the ice. We would have had no problems.

SECTION TEN   *I Proved Myself*

I had only been in the army, training in Nome, for one month when there was an accident that broke my leg. I was helping to unload a transport ship, moving some lumber. The sling slipped out from under some timbers and the lumber fell on me. I was put into the hospital in Nome but the doctors did not set the fracture properly and infection set in. That month the Japanese invasion started in the Aleutian Islands and the doctors were trying to make room for wounded soldiers. So they transferred quite a few patients, including me, to Barnes General Hospital in Vancouver, Washington. By this time gangrene had set into my leg.

The doctors at Barnes said that if I had been sent sooner,they could have tried to save my leg, but it was too late. So they had to do three operations to amputate my leg. It was very painful.

I was sent down to Bushnell General Hospital in Brigham City, Utah to be fitted with a wooden leg. I was there about five months. I felt that I wanted to die. All my preparation to be a good hunter was lost. I had lost everything. I could not go out hunting in the moving ice any more. The Bering Sea ice moves *all* the time — north, south, east and west — and it is very dangerous. It is a very dangerous place to be even with two legs.

After I was discharged from the army and sent back home, my cousin made me crutches. I was just completely disappointed at that time, frustrated and depressed. Most of the people who had a very close relationship to me said that they had lost somebody who would have been a successful hunter. They had tried to prepare me especially to be a polar bear hunter. That is partly what all the running was for, to build my muscles to run after polar bears when they tried to get away. And I had lost that. I was twenty-one years old and I had lost everything.

I decided that I would hunt anyway. What else could I do? I made myself heavier crutches so that I could walk on the ice. Starting out, I tried to hunt mostly on the shore ice because the ice was not moving. I was able to carry my rifle and my hunting bag over my shoulders and to move through the shore ice using my crutches.

One day the weather was really nice, the current was not moving fast, and the wind was calm. When the wind is calm, the current is slow. I went out hunting and I got myself a seal. I felt pretty good about it. I had gone out into the moving ice and I had been successful hunting. I started to drag the seal toward the shore ice. I took a line from my hunting bag, tied it around the seal and around my waist, and headed home. I did not get very far. A lead opened up in front of me, open water, and I fell in, inside the moving ice. I could not get out. Good thing there was somebody nearby. I hollered at him and he came running and pulled me out.

Another time I went out hunting on the moving ice and I lost my rifle. I was catching a seal and I had some of my equipment out near its breathing hole. My hunting bag and my rifle were some distance away. The ice cracked between my rifle and myself and I could not jump it; I could not go over to get my rifle. The lead was only about two or three feet wide. Anybody else could have jumped it but I could not. So I made a really long walk around the lead to try to get my hunting bag at least, but the ice cracked again and the rifle sank.

The hunting bag was floating in the water but I could not get it. It would have been saved if I had not been handicapped. So I said to myself finally, "If I try to go out hunting on crutches, one day I will not come back. It is too dangerous."

So I built myself a little skin boat. My nephew, my brother's son, and my brother, helped me make the wooden frame and some of the women of the village sewed the split walrus hides to cover the frame. I thought I could hunt from a skin boat more safely than by walking on crutches. Whenever the north wind blew, I hunted in the open water on the south side of the village. That way I started getting more seals. I had used a kayak to hunt seals before my accident, but I could not balance myself anymore in a kayak. I had more weight on my good leg and less weight on my wooden leg. In order to balance my kayak I had to lean towards one side and it was very hard on my back. So I never used the kayak anymore. I used the little skin boat; it was about sixteen feet long.

Even though I became handicapped, people at King Island tried to be helpful to me in every way that they could. One winter my nephew, my brother and I went out hunting on the east side of the island. We went out until we could not go out any farther because the area was closed with ice and the skin boat could not go through. We pulled our little skin boat on top of the ice. I looked north and I saw some object above the pressure ridge of ice off in the distance. And above the object were two ravens flying.

Now when I was young, my mother used to tell me that whenever my father saw two ravens playing with something on the ice, that meant that an animal was present, maybe a fox or maybe a polar bear! And I saw those two ravens go down and go up and go down and go up. I just kept looking where they went down in the distance and I saw that object, and I knew right away that it was a polar bear. I told my brother and my nephew, "There is a polar bear coming toward us. Maybe we should pull our skin boat up some more so that it will not be carried away by the ice." So we pulled it up a little way from the water.

We went over behind the big pressure ridges and we hid. We saw that there were three polar bears, a mother and two cubs almost the same size as the mother. Every time we looked, they had come closer. They could not see us, only our skin boat. They may have thought the boat was a seal or a walrus. Finally, as they started to move away from us, we each took aim at one polar bear and we shot all three.

My mother was still living then and when we came home she asked me, "Did you kill that polar bear, son?"

I said, "Yes," and she began crying for joy. She thought I was not able to kill a polar bear because I was handicapped, but I managed to get one. We used the meat for food and we sold the furs.

We had a polar bear dance about one week later. We gave away food, rawhide and furs from the animals. I was store manager at the village then and I had ordered an ice cream maker for that year, to make ice cream the white man's way. That is the first time we served ice cream at a polar bear dance. And the next day one of my really close relatives said, "Paul, you should get another polar bear so that we can have some more ice cream."

I think I killed every type of animal at King Island — seal, walrus, polar bear, birds. I did what I had prepared for before I became handicapped. My preparation to be a good hunter was not wasted at all. When I started to hunt from my little skin boat, I could compare with the other hunters. I never tried to be a great hunter but only to compete with the others. But I proved myself to be a hunter — not a handicapped person — but a hunter.

The City

My wife and I lived on King Island until 1956 when we moved to Nome. We lived in Nome for twelve years. I did some ivory carving, some janitorial work to support my family. And I was still hunting. The people on King Island had started moving to Nome in 1948 to get jobs and because of medical problems. No one had travelled much prior to that time, except in the service; then tourism came in and offered us a chance to travel. We were good dancers on King Island and the airlines offered to take us stateside, to promote their business. They took Native dancers out to Seattle, Los Angeles, San Francisco, New York and Washington, D.C. The airlines encouraged us to dance for the tourists in Nome and in Anchorage.

We moved to town because of health problems in the family also. At the turn of the century, the major health problem was tuberculosis. Our people picked it up from whalers and from people in Nome. It was a deadly disease for Alaskan life. A lot of us went to Nome because some of our family members were hospitalized at the Native sanitorium at Mount Edgecumbe in Southeast Alaska or at Orangeside in Seattle. We had to be in town in order to have better communication with them.

After some of the people had left King Island, the government forced the rest of them out. The Bureau of Indian Affairs is the agency that is supposed to be responsible for Native Americans. At the end the BIA condemned the school and did not replace it. The families with kids had to move to Nome in order to have some sort of education, a different education from the Native way. The last family moved from King Island in 1969. Since then no family has moved back because there is no teacher. The only people who go back are ones that are single or whose children are all grown up. The law says you have to have an education.

Also, one of the big excuses the Bureau of Indian Affairs had for moving us away from King Island was danger from rocks. They told the King Islanders, "There's a big rock on the top of the village. Experts say it is going to come down any time and the school and some of the houses are in its path." The rock is still up there. It never rolled down. The BIA tried to make all kinds of excuses for locking the island. I do not know what the government is trying to do for Native people. A lot of times, I just reject the idea of the BIA.

In 1967 I came down to Anchorage for a meeting of Alaska Legal Services, to represent the northwestern part of the state. I was hired by the Alaska Centennial people to work in tourism. My wife and I decided we could make a living here. We go back to Nome and King Island in the summer time.

After the Centennial I worked for the Alaska Native Welcome Center and then the State of Alaska as an employment interviewer. After that, on the Trans-Alaska Pipeline, I was a site counselor at a pump station. I worked with the superintendent, supervisors and foremen on Native hire as a middle man between the supervisors and the Native workers to help communication. I worked for nearly a year at the Seward Skill Center as a recreation director. Then for ten years I was employed at the Cook Inlet Native Association as a cultural coordinator. I work with our Native people as they adjust to urban life.

The influence of this modern society is very confusing for our Native people. On the one hand we are told that we have to go to school to make a living, more income, cash for our pockets to buy better things for ourselves. In order to be somebody, we are encouraged to finish grade school, finish high school, finish college, so that we will really know how to do all the paper work. I wish that I had been given a good clear picture of what schooling would provide me in the future.

But when we go to school, we lose our own culture. All kinds of concerned persons say that we should retain our culture, but to do that we have to go back into the old ways. The only income we get from Native culture is food for our families. In the Native way, everything is given by nature. We have to learn to compete with Mother Nature, and nobody knows what Mother Nature is going to do. Even down in California there are droughts and nothing grows. Even the modern society cannot compete with Mother Nature. To live the Native way, we must have instruction or we will be lost. We will be dead.

If I really wanted to go back to King Island, I would go back. But my family says no. The family has to make decisions also. The man does not have to make decisions all the time. If my family members think they can make a better living here in Anchorage, I go along with them even though I want to go back to Nome, closer to King Island. If I could take my whole family to King Island, I would have to reteach them how to live by Mother Nature. But my kids do not want to go back because there is no income, there is no money involved when they go back to Native culture. My two girls went to the University of Alaska. They have good jobs here in Anchorage and they cannot use the Native ways which I want to teach them.

I have tried to integrate myself into the working system of this modern society. I am a school dropout and I do not know much about writing or about business. But the good thing is that I have been taught the Native ways since I was a kid, and I can earn an income by teaching about it. I have been saying that a lot of young people are trapped right in the middle. They are dropouts and they cannot find any kind of work, because they do not have any experience at all. I am a little bit luckier than others because I have knowledge enough to do something in the Native culture, like dancing, carving, telling stories and explaining about Native ways.

What the Bureau of Indian Affairs should do from the beginning is give young people the whole picture of this modern society. If a young person wants to integrate — if a young person wants to be a plumber, for example — the BIA should send him to a trade school. But a snag we get into is that the whole family is so tight knit that the parents do not give their consent to the young person to go away to learn a trade. A lot of families feel this way. I feel that way and my mother felt that way. I should encourage my kids to go further in their schooling because that is the only way they can make a good living. There is a lot of competition when people are seeking jobs; this society will only accept somebody who has education enough to do some kind of work.

The biggest mistake the federal government hands out is the welfare system. We did not have a welfare system in my early days but somehow we got by through the winters. If you want to make a living, you have to go out there and work at something that should provide you with an income. The welfare system is a hand-out. The government gives it to you to buy something for yourself and relax at your home because the government is going to take care of you. In that way the government makes our people lazy. It says, "Here's the money, here's a thousand dollars. You can buy yourself a snowmobile or a speed boat or whatever, and then relax because additional money will come to you each month." Why should I work? That is a really bad influence, the hand-out from the federal government, because it takes away pride from the Native tribes.

The United States government should talk to our elders and see which is the best way to teach or direct the King Island people. The only things the schools teach now are the ABC's and arithmetic. They do not bring up the problems we are going to encounter during our lifetimes. When we try to integrate ourselves into the urban center, the impact is so great and very hard to understand—the business part of the urban life—that we cannot go anywhere. Our kids have been changed so much in the modern system that they do not listen to the elders when the elders say something to them. The kids do not accept anymore.

The government should work with the parents, by explaining more about how the modern system works. When the government first came into the villages, Native people did not have any lawyers, state troopers, policemen, jails or correctional centers. The government started to influence us, telling us we required these agencies which were not required before, because we had our own system. I did not see any child abuse in our village when I was young. We did not have any alcohol or drug problems when I was young. We did not have divorces.

We could integrate both systems if the government sat down with us and made plans to educate our children the modern way and the village way, to satisfy both sides. The teachers must sit down with us, and the lawyers and the state troopers and the policemen, and all the other government officials. We can teach them the Eskimo ways because they are the best ways for our people. And we can make a contribution to modern American society.

NOTE   Paul Tiulana continues to contribute to the welfare of his people and his country. In 1983 he was named "Man of the Year" by the Alaska Federation of Natives, a statewide organization representing all of the Alaska Native regions and cultures. In 1984 he traveled to Washington, D.C. to receive a National Heritage Fellowship Award, presented by the chairman of the National Endowment for the Arts. The award states:

The Folk Arts Program of the National Endowment for the Arts recognizes Paul Tiulana as a Master Traditional Artist who has contributed to the shaping of our artistic traditions and to preserving the cultural diversity of the United States.

The American Festival of Arts sent Paul and his wife, Clara, to London, England in 1985 to demonstrate ethnic arts at the Museum of Mankind. Prince Philip met Paul and Clara at the Museum and received gifts on behalf of Queen Elizabeth from the Native people of Alaska.

Here I am, just coming in from hunting. I was seventeen years old when the picture was taken. I was dragging a seal that day. That is how I got the icicles all over. The wide leather oogruk band was used for dragging the seal. I was also carrying a harpoon line. The pouch is a shell case made of wolverine head skin and spotted seal skin.

This is King Island. It is in the Bering Sea, thirty-five miles from Cape Douglas on the Alaskan mainland, and ninety miles from Nome. The island is two and a half miles long. The village faces south. It is the best place in the world to lose weight and get away from city life.

This is the whole village. The biggest building is the church. The larger frame houses were built by Father Hubbard in 1938–39 for his staff members. They belonged to the church. On the lower left is the school house. On the far right of the picture the doorway dug into the hill is the entrance of the clubhouse where we did our ivory carving, built our hunting equipment, and dried our sealskins in the winter time.

Our houses were built of wood. Each living quarters was about ten feet by ten feet. The roof and the back part of the house were covered with walrus hide to insulate the house from the wind. Out in front seal skins and a polar bear hide are weather dried and bleached.

Ignatius Annayuk is eating a murre egg. We collected murre eggs in the middle of June. The murres laid their eggs right on the cliffs in little nooks and on rock ridges.

Frances is my half-sister. She is holding a king crab.
We used to tie bait — young bullheads cut in half — on
a line made of baleen from the mouth of a whale. We
put a sinker on the line and dropped it. When the crab
grabbed it, we pulled it up.

Frances is married to an outside person from the
lower forty-eight states.

This is Quagluk holding bullheads, bottom fish. Bullheads were caught through the ice with the Eskimo fishing hook and baleen fishing line. The hook has three pieces in it: one stone (which could be a sparkle stone), one lead, and a piece of walrus ivory with a copper or brass hook.

Aloysius Ayak is hooking a puffin chick from the rocks. These chicks are about eight or ten inches long and fat and really tender, good to eat. They are caught in the latter part of September.

This is Ahnatook holding a baby seal brought in by her father, John Ollanna. The seal pup was born the first or second week of April. He brought the seal home so that she could play with it for awhile. Then it was killed. The fur was used for trimming moccasins and parkas.

These boys are sliding down the hill to clean the hair on the polar bear skin. This was in December or January, when we had about six hours of daylight.

Bernard Kasignoc is preparing his kayak for spring hunting. He is working on top of his house. Bernard was both a cross-cousin and a partner's cousin to me. Mostly he was a cross-cousin to me at King Island, that is, he used to tease me. But when we admitted someone from the mainland who was a cross-cousin to both of us, then he became my partner's cousin and we worked together.

The hunter is taking off his pulling harness as he gets home. This is a two-kayak sled used for pulling the kayaks over rough ice. The kayak is fully equipped with a seal poke, a harpoon, a harpoon holder, a paddle, and sticks for pulling meat out from inside the kayak.

The men of King Island are making a well inside the skin boat, for an outboard motor. Several people have to help because the boat weighs so much. They are probably talking about the day's hunting.

Here is my mother, Annie Kattac, picking some flowers. She cooked these sour tasting greens in water and put them in barrels. In the winter time she took them out and mixed them with seal oil and reindeer fat.

This is my wife, Clara, when she was about eighteen. She is coming back from the underground shelter where we kept our meat that should not have been exposed to the sun. The shelter is made out of rocks and wood and some whalebone.

Our parents had to pick our wives, our husbands. Mostly wives. If the parents thought a young man could support a family, they would allow the marriage. That is how we got married. I was dating my wife before my mother chose her. I would invite her to a dance. We could go after a girl and catch her. We just played outside and went for walks. We did not like to show ourselves to the public because if some of our cross-cousins saw us, they would tease us the next day.

This is my mother-in-law. She and my father-in-law were really nice to me. I did whatever they wanted me to do and in return they gave me anything I wanted. When I first was married to my wife, we were just ready to go to Nome. My father-in-law said to me, "When you go to Nome, do not go with bad people." That meant not to go in the bars. In Eskimo culture we cannot refuse anything that has been said by our in-laws, so I stopped drinking for twenty years. I was a heavy drinker before I married. I started drinking just before I went into the service, in World War II. Good thing I stopped drinking because otherwise my kids might have worn torn clothes and had nothing to eat.

My mother-in-law provided everything for us—clothing and instruction and babysitting. And my in-laws provided a lot of help to my wife and my mother.

Twenty-two King Islanders are going to Nome on Nereruk's boat. The trip took thirteen hours with an outboard motor. The sails are ready in case the winds are right. An empty seal poke is hanging over the side.

This picture shows the pressure ridges formed by the current on the south side of the island. Some of the pressure ridges are twelve feet high and twenty feet deep under the ice. The dots on the center left of the picture may be some people ice fishing for bottom fish and crabs.

To climb from the upper houses down to the ice takes about five minutes when you are young, ten to fifteen minutes when you are old. The island slopes at a forty-five degree angle.

These are the hunting kayaks left down on the shore ice after the hunters came in from hunting. They never took the kayaks off the sleds because they were going to use them again the next morning. The lances with hooks were used to pull the kayaks up against the edge of the ice. They were also used to test young ice.

James Ahrusak is wearing full winter hunting equipment. The wolverine ruff protects him from freezing cold. He has his spear and his walking stick and a harpoon line around his neck. The white parka is for camouflage from animals on the ice.

These four men went out hunting early in March on the eastern side of King Island. On the left is Stanislau Muktoyuk, the second is Joachim Koyuk, the third is Phillip Tatayuna, and I am on the right. It was a really good hunting day for us because all of us have a seal. The rings around our necks are called spearlines. They were attached to our necks when we speared the big bearded seal or the walrus. Our spears were used for killing animals and also for testing the thickness of the ice and cutting through ice ridges. On our backs we are carrying rifles in bleached sealskin bags, and our hunting bags made out of seal float sealskin. We carried our necessary survival items inside our hunting bags. Our snowshoes were tied behind our hunting bags.

In the background are pressure ridges where the current has pushed the ice against the island. Most of the ice is underneath the surface, sometimes all the way to the bottom of the ocean.

*The men are dragging a walrus skin. The skin proba-
bly weighed about six hundred pounds. They dragged
it close to the island so that the women could dress it
for a skin boat cover. At King Island we did not have
dog teams for hauling because the ice was too rough
to use a dog team.*

Charles Mayac and John Alvanna are holding seal poke floats and harpoons. The men are cross-cousins. Charles is my wife, Clara's, oldest brother. John is both a cross-cousin and a partner's cousin to me.

Phillip Tatayuna is holding a walrus stomach which would be cut up to make Eskimo drum heads. It was blown up to dry so that it would not wrinkle. Phillip was my cross-cousin. He used to work with my father before he died. After my father died, Phillip went out hunting with my uncle. When I grew up and I wanted to build a skinboat, Phillip helped me build one. He went out hunting with me. He treated me as my father would have.

John Alvanna is putting rawhide cut from the skin of a young oogruk, or big bearded seal, on a large wooden spool. The women did the skin-sewing but the men cut the rawhide strips.

Father LaFortune was our priest for fifteen years. He rarely left the island. If the old folks decided to stay on the island when the younger villagers went to the mainland in the summer, Father LaFortune stayed with them.

The "Christ the King" is made out of bronze. It was placed at the top of the island and could be seen from the village, from the sea and from the air.

My first cousin, Ellanna, is with her daughter, Cecilia. Ellanna used to make mukluks, or boots, for me. In order to return the services, when I grew up, I gave whole seals to her.

Ursalus Ellanna is cutting up a walrus flipper. She is my second cousin. She was from Mary's Igloo, married to my cross-cousin, Frank Ellanna. The walrus flippers are cooked, boiled, and eaten with seal oil.

Susrak is cutting a female walrus hide for boats, using a woman's knife called an ulu. Her waterproof boots, or mukluks, are fancy — made of sealskin with bleached sealskin trim.

Susrak was a housewife. Her first husband was Soolook and she had four children with him. He may have died of tuberculosis. Her second husband was Nerizoc and they had one daughter.

Qawaliak is making a cribbage board from walrus ivory. When he was a boy, his mother took him over to a running stream in the fall of the year and she put his hands in cold water for a few minutes to make them tough. It worked. He could cut seals in the winter without mittens.

He was also known for the Eskimo songs that he composed for the village.

Robert Nuyakok was a kind of village doctor who set dislocated joints and massaged sore areas on the body, loosening the tissues and nerves. He was also an ivory carver. He was married and had two boys. When we had contests of accuracy at throwing stones or pebbles, he could hit any object.

Theresa Mayac is packing some meat in an oogruk hide carrying bag. She was originally from the village of Mary's Igloo. She was raised at the Catholic mission at Pilgrim's Springs because both her parents died when she was small. She married a King Island man.

John Ollanna, my uncle, is holding paddles and harpoon lines for his skinboat. He had a skin disease and his face turned white. Then he burned in the sun. Sometimes he wore a cotton scarf over his nose and mouth. He was a good hunter and a good teacher for me. He became the first president of the King Island Council, which was formed in 1934.

This is what we called the Half Mask Dance. The dancer is my uncle, John Ollanna. In the background there are nine singers and drummers. The dance was kind of comical, to make the people laugh. It was held underneath the church.

This picture shows the first part of the Wolf Dance. There are five men and five women dancing. The Wolf Dance has a very long story: it tells about a wolf presented by an eagle to a hunter. The mother of the eagle is upset because she has lost her son.

The gloves are made of sealskin with ivory rattles and polar bear fur trim. The headdresses are made of eagles' feathers. The gloves and headdresses were handed down through generations.

These men are building a new skinboat in the month of May. The frame is made of driftwood tied together with rawhide. The man on the right is Charlie Tigmeak.

The women of the village are making a cover for a skinboat. Split walrus hide is used. The outside layer is used for the cover. Three or four skins are sewn together with waterproof stitches. We use the inside layer of the hide for the inside of the skinboat frame, so that our belongings will not get wet.

This is a party for a polar bear hunter. Leo Kunnuk is giving away agutaq, or Eskimo ice cream. The old man on the right, Matthew Anasungok, is making up a new polar bear song. He put in words about where the man hunted the polar bear, whether the man killed the bear on new ice or young ice, and the kind of activities the polar bear had.

This is my Aunt Nereruk. She is babysitting for her daughter, packing her grandson. She was the oldest child in my father's family. She had two daughters who were married. She lived by herself on King Island when her husband died. Then she moved in with her older daughter in Nome, until she died.

Aunt Nereruk was a really strong woman. She could pack a two hundred pound walrus skin, even when she was carrying a baby.

THE PHOTOGRAPHER: FATHER BERNARD R. HUBBARD, S.J.

Father Bernard Hubbard dedicated a major part of his amazing long life to study, exploration and religious service in Alaska. His photographs of the King Island people form a relatively small but especially beautiful part of the work he did.

Bernard Rosencrans Hubbard was born in San Francisco in 1888. His father, a college professor, bought land in the Big Basin Redwood area south of San Francisco when his son was ten years old. Bernard began to explore the woods and mountains of California at a time when travel to the country involved a sometimes wild ride on a Calistoga stagecoach pulled by six horses.

At the age of twenty, Bernard Hubbard entered the Jesuit Order at Los Gatos, California. Five years later he was teaching Latin, English, mathematics and ancient history in a Jesuit college in east Los Angeles. He also coached baseball and football.

Next, the Order sent him to Mount St. Michael's House of Philosophy in Spokane, Washington. Outside Spokane he studied sections of a 200,000 square mile field of lava beds. He accompanied another priest, a scientist, on expeditions through the Columbia River Basin in eastern Washington, areas of Idaho and Montana, Glacier Park and the Yellowstone region in Wyoming.

Father Hubbard made many trips to Europe. He studied theology in Innsbruck, Austria and spent his holidays and summer vacations exploring alpine peaks and glaciers. His guides named him "Gletscher Pfarrer" which translates to Glacier Priest, the title he carried all his life.

Father Hubbard made his first of many trips to Alaska in 1927 to explore the Mendenhall and Taku glaciers. He brought Santa Clara University students with him on subsequent trips to Alaska. The results of these expeditions and investigations made Father Hubbard's reputation as an expert on Alaska—its glaciers, volcanoes, weather conditions and some of its people. The team took still and motion pictures which Father Hubbard showed to hundreds of thousands of people in nationwide lecture tours over the years. He published a stream of articles and two books, *Mush You Malemutes* (1932) and *Cradle of the Storms* (1935).

On his many trips to Alaska, Father Hubbard always carried his Mass kit. He packed it on his back or included it with other supplies on dog sleds. He stated late in his life that "Daily Mass and breviary meant everything to me all my life, and in all my traveling the schedules had to be made out so that neither the privilege nor the obligation would be endangered."

In 1938 and 1939 Father Hubbard lived on King Island. He continued his glacier research and captured the King Island people on film. The King Islanders took him on a 2,000 mile open-water trip by skinboat. He was able to supervise the erection of the bronze statue entitled "Christ the King" at the top of the island mountain. There the statue could serve as an invitation to peace between two hemispheres. This was the realization of a dream of Father LaFortune, King Island's resident priest for over twenty years. King Island carvers presented Father Hubbard with two ivory carvings of "Christ the King." He took these with Eskimo greetings to Pope Pius XII.

Father Hubbard enjoyed a cooperative relationship with the United States military throughout his career. The Air Force and the Coast Guard brought his supplies into the Alaska wilderness. Air Force pilots saw to it that he was in a position to film the steam and lava and the ice and snow of active and inactive volcanoes on the Aleutian Chain. The Glacier Priest lectured to American soldiers on the European front during World War II. He counseled with General Patton and General Mac-Arthur.

At the age of 67, Father Hubbard suffered a stroke and was paralyzed. Three years later, he recovered and returned again to Alaska. He climbed in and out of boats with some difficulty, held his movie camera with his limp right hand and worked it with his good left hand.

Father Hubbard's home base was Santa Clara University. He lived in Santa Clara during the latter part of his life and deposited there the vast collections of data, photographs and motion pictures created during his explorations and adventures. He was planning yet another summer trip to Alaska when he died in 1962.

This biographical sketch of Father Hubbard is based upon an article provided by Santa Clara University with permission.